Literature Review

THE EQUITY RISK PREMIUM: A CONTEXTUAL LITERATURE REVIEW

Laurence B. Siegel

CFA Institute Research Foundation

Statement of Purpose

The CFA Institute Research Foundation is a not-for-profit organization established to promote the development and dissemination of relevant research for investment practitioners worldwide.

Cover Image Photo Credit: wildpixel/Getty Images

ISBN 978-1-944960-31-5

Editorial Staff

Stephen Smith
Editor

Cindy Maisannes
Manager, Publications Technology and Production

Tracy Dinning
Senior Publishing Technology Specialist

Contents

CE Qualified Activity CFA Institute

This publication qualifies for 0.5 CE credits under the guidelines of the CFA Institute Continuing Education Program.

The Equity Risk Premium: A Contextual Literature Review

Laurence B. Siegel

Laurence B. Siegel is the Gary P. Brinson director of research at the CFA Institute Research Foundation, Charlottesville, Virginia.

The equity risk premium (ERP), or equity premium, is the difference in expected or realized return between an equity index and a reference asset,[1] where the latter is usually a bond or bill portfolio considered to be "riskless."[2] In the modern literature and in investment management practice, ERP usually means "*expected* ERP," and I will stick to that convention, reserving the phrase "realized ERP" for any backward-looking or historical measure.

The ERP is widely acknowledged as the most important variable in finance. It is useful

- for determining what returns to expect from each major asset class and from portfolios of securities or asset classes;
- in life-cycle and retirement planning (estimating how much to save and invest in the hope of achieving a given standard of living in retirement); and
- as a component of the opportunity cost of capital or required rate of return in corporate finance.

An estimate of the ERP is required for essentially all asset allocation models and is central to the practice of investment management and asset/liability management. ERP estimates thus strongly affect the asset allocation decisions of individual investors and institutional investors, including pensions, endowment funds, foundations, and insurance companies.

[1]Occasionally, the reference asset is "inflation"—that is, a hypothetical asset returning the rate of consumer price inflation as measured by some index.

[2]I would argue that no asset is completely riskless.

Approaches to Estimating the ERP

This review is organized by theme, roughly in the order in which the themes first appeared in the literature. Approaches to estimating the ERP fall into three broad categories:

1. Methods based on a dividend discount model (DDM), earnings discount model, or cash-flow-to-the-investor discount model: forward-looking methods with their roots in discounted cash flow (DCF) analysis, wherein the value of an asset is regarded as the present value of the cash flows the asset is expected to generate.
2. Methods based on extrapolating past trends, in particular the spread between realized stock and bond or cash returns, into the future: retrospective methods.
3. Methods based on a macroeconomic model of the way that investors require compensation for risk.

In past literature, these have been called, respectively, supply, equilibrium, and demand models.[3] The DDM is a supply model because it focuses on ways that companies generate cash with which to reward investors. The macroeconomic model is a demand model because it asks what excess return investors need to induce them to take equity risk. The retrospective method can be regarded as an equilibrium model because it relies on prices at which the market actually traded, reflecting the intersection of supply and demand curves.

Earliest Estimates. The earliest estimates of the ERP were derived by estimating the expected return on an equity portfolio using the DDM and then subtracting the expected return or yield on the riskless asset. This "DDM approach," which made a comeback at the end of the 20th century, is the method most widely used today.

Future Equals Past. The next step was taken by researchers who measured the realized ERP, asserting that the realized ERP was the best estimate of the expected ERP. In their view, neither the amount of risk in the market nor the "price of risk" (the return investors require and expect to receive for

[3]Roger G. Ibbotson, "The Equity Risk Premium," in *Rethinking the Equity Risk Premium*, edited by P. Brett Hammond, Jr., Martin L. Leibowitz, and Laurence B. Siegel (Charlottesville, VA: CFA Institute Research Foundation, 2011): https://www.cfapubs.org/doi/pdf/10.2470/rf.v2011.n4.8. This work describes the supply and demand models. In other works and in conversations, Roger Ibbotson has characterized the retrospective method as an equilibrium model.

taking a given amount of risk) changes much over time; that is, the return-generating process for equities (in excess of the riskless rate) is stable or stationary. This method is called the future-equals-past approach.

The future-equals-past approach suffers from the following flaw: The higher the market rises, the higher the estimate of future returns given by the method. This outcome is contrary to intuition, which would lead one to expect a low return (on any asset) if one pays a high going-in price for the asset. Consider, for example, a bond: If the past return is 10% per year because interest rates have fallen from, say, 5% at the beginning of the holding period to 1% at the end, is the expected return 10% or 1%? It is the latter.

In addition, the future-equals-past approach assumes that markets are fairly priced and does not allow for the possibility that they are not. This possibility became a primary focus of research once the future-equals-past method lost its preeminence.

The Macro Approach or "Equity Premium Puzzle." Starting around 1985, academics began to question why the realized ERP—and apparently also the expected ERP—was so large when certain aspects of macroeconomic theory suggested it should be much smaller. That is, other trade-offs between risk and reward in the economy implied that investors did not require nearly as large a risk premium as they had been getting.

This "equity premium puzzle" literature, while extensive and contentious, turned out to be something of a dead end because the ERP, while arguably smaller than it once was, is still much larger than the puzzle literature says it should be. I nevertheless take this literature seriously and document it in the "Equity Premium 'Puzzle'" section below.

The DDM Counterrevolution. A substantial innovation occurred in the 1980s when several researchers found the ERP to be *time varying*. This literature spawned a mountain of research on the time-series behavior of equity market valuation measures, particularly price-to-earnings ratios (P/Es).

The P/E-related research asks, among other questions, what the best definition of "earnings" is for forecasting future returns. The cyclically adjusted price-to-earnings ratio (CAPE), which smoothes earnings data by averaging them over long periods, typically 10 years, has become the most popular measure. (P/E and CAPE are relevant to ERP estimation because if the ERP is time varying, these statistics provide a way to get continuously updated measures of the expected return on equities; one can then subtract bond or bill yields to arrive at the ERP itself.) This thread, which is called "time-varying premia," continues today as the predominant trend in ERP research.

A branch of the time-varying ERP tree asks what, besides earnings, might accurately measure the desirability of an equity investment. The most important alternative is payout, or "cash flow to the investor"—that is, dividends plus other cash flows, such as those from share buybacks.

Other Works. While most of the work that has been done on the ERP relates to the United States, the underlying issues are the same everywhere. I review literature that extends this work to international markets.

Finally, I list and comment briefly on other literature reviews, compilations, and aggregative works.

First Stirrings

Edgar Smith, in 1924, seemed to intuit the equity risk premium.[4] He presented evidence that stocks had high returns, realized or expected (he did not make the distinction), relative to other, primarily fixed-income assets. In 1938, the Harvard professor John Burr Williams was the first to state that the value of a firm is the discounted present value of all of its future dividends.[5] He wrote, "Earnings are only a means to an end [dividends], and the means should not be mistaken for the end" (p. 47).

Williams's discounted cash flow formula, familiar to all business students, represents the origin of risk premium thinking because the discount rate, in order to be useful for valuing stocks, must be a risky discount rate that is higher than the riskless rate by an amount (the equity risk premium) that compensates the investor fairly, but not more than fairly, for the risk of the stock.

In 1956, Myron Gordon and Eli Shapiro, building on Williams's work, formalized the notion of a risky discount rate and equated the expected return on an equity with the "required rate of profit."[6] This principle is the foundation of corporate finance, which asserts that the market for an asset (say, an equity) is in equilibrium when the expected return on the asset equals the required return—that is, the return that investors demand as fair compensation for the asset's risk.

Future Equals Past

But these early works did not lead directly to estimates of the ERP that were practicable for asset allocation, capital budgeting, and other uses to which the

[4]Edgar Lawrence Smith, *Common Stocks as Long Term Investments* (New York: Macmillan, 1924; Eastford, CT: Martino Fine Books, 2012).

[5]John Burr Williams, *The Theory of Investment Value* (Cambridge, MA: Harvard University Press, 1938).

[6]Myron J. Gordon and Eli Shapiro, "Capital Equipment Analysis: The Required Rate of Profit," *Management Science*, vol. 3, no. 1 (1956): 102–110.

premium is now put. Ibbotson and Sinquefield (1976) made explicit estimates of the ERP by calculating, as far back in history as high-quality data allowed, the difference between the realized total returns on an equity index and the realized total returns on a bond or bill (cash) portfolio. The logic was that over time, investors conform their expectations to that which is actually realizable, so that the historical return (in excess of the riskless rate) is a fair or equilibrium estimate of the return (in excess of the riskless rate) that investors should expect going forward.

Ibbotson and Sinquefield decomposed historical returns on an equity index into a part attributable to the riskless rate and a part attributable to the equity premium. The arithmetic mean of the equity premium part is assumed to be stationary—that is, the same in the future as in the past. Thus, if equities had beaten riskless Treasury bills by an arithmetic mean margin of 7% a year over the historical measurement period (which was usually 1926 through the then-current time), then equities were forecast to beat bills by the same amount in the future.

The arithmetic mean expected total return on equities was then calculated as the sum of the forward-looking riskless rate (i.e., the yield on riskless bills or bonds) and the arithmetic mean expected ERP.

Reflecting on Ibbotson and Sinquefield's pioneering work, I wrote:

> Hadn't anyone before . . . Ibbotson and . . . Sinquefield . . . estimated the equity risk premium? Of course the thought had occurred to many, but the preexisting methodology—to use a kind of Dividend Discount Model (DDM) for the aggregate of all stocks in the market—gave forecasts, or estimates of the *ex ante* or expected risk premium, not backward looks at history. Hindsight showed that DDM-based forecasts had been much too low. A typical DDM estimate of the forward-looking, or expected, equity risk premium over bonds was in the range of 2 to 3 percent. In contrast, Ibbotson [and Sinquefield] showed that stocks had out-returned intermediate-term Treasury bonds by much more, 5.4 percent, using 1926 to 1979 as the measurement period. (p. xii)[7]

Ibbotson and Sinquefield's work was tremendously influential, led to the establishment of a firm (Ibbotson Associates) that would later be acquired by Morningstar, and was updated in yearbook form by Morningstar until 2015 and by Duff & Phelps thereafter (Ibbotson, Grabowski, Harrington, and Nunes 2017).[8] Their method is still the way that many finance professors,

[7]Laurence B. Siegel, foreword to *Frontiers of Modern Asset Allocation*, by Paul D. Kaplan (Hoboken, NJ: John Wiley & Sons, 2011).

[8]Starting about 2015, Morningstar discontinued "future-equals-past" estimates of the ERP in its updates of the Ibbotson yearbook, noting that DDM-type forecasts are more accurate and more theoretically justifiable.

investment management and sales executives, and others make their long-run forecasts. However, over roughly the last quarter century, other methods—principally based on a forward-looking discounted cash flow (DCF) model, such as the DDM—have become competitive and even dominant.

As noted, the future-equals-past method was the principal way of estimating the ERP for a long time after Ibbotson and Sinquefield's early studies. However, a 1984 paper, which was mostly ignored at the time but which would later become influential, called into question the relevance of this method's forecasts. Jeffrey Diermeier, who would later serve as president and CEO of CFA Institute, wrote the paper with Roger Ibbotson and myself.

We argued that (1) corporate earnings could not indefinitely grow faster than the overall economy, or there would eventually be nothing left for labor, government, and other claimants, and (2) P/E could not rise indefinitely either. As a result, the growth rate of the economy—that is, of GDP—is the hypothetical upper limit of the very-long-term rate of price return on equities. In addition to that return, the investor receives dividends. See Diermeier, Ibbotson, and Siegel (1984).

This argument asserts that a DDM is the right way to think about the ERP. While this idea remained dormant for some time, it would constitute the main thrust of ERP estimation in the 1990s and thereafter.

The Equity Premium "Puzzle"

In the 1980s, while practitioners were debating whether the ERP was low (3% or 4%, as suggested by DDM methods) or high (more than 5%, as obtained by extrapolating historical data), a group of academics were wondering why the ERP was not trivially more than zero. Mehra and Prescott (1985) described a "puzzle" whereby the ERP realized over the period 1889–1978 (or any other similarly long period, such as 1926 to the present) was too high, *by at least an order of magnitude,* to be explained by standard "general equilibrium" or "macroeconomic" asset-pricing models.

Using these models, such a high premium can be explained only by a very high coefficient of risk aversion, one in the range of 30 to 40. (The risk aversion parameter describes a given individual's trade-off between the amount of risk taken and the amount of additional return he or she requires as compensation for taking that risk.) Risk aversion parameters observed in other aspects of financial behavior are around 1. So, Mehra and Prescott argued, either the model used to describe investors' behavior is flawed or equity investors have received a much higher return than they expected.

The asset-pricing models referenced by Mehra and Prescott (1985) are called "macroeconomic" because they originated in that specialty but also, more importantly, to distinguish them from asset-pricing models commonly used in investment finance—such as the capital asset pricing model, the three-factor Fama–French model, and arbitrage pricing theory—that are silent on the absolute size of the risk premium (in fact, requiring it as an input) and that distinguish instead among the expected *relative* returns on specific securities or portfolios.

Research on the question of why the realized equity premium was so large can be divided into three broad categories: (1) studies alleging bias in the historical data, (2) studies suggesting improvements in the macroeconomic model, and (3) studies that raise behavioral finance, life-cycle, and other issues.

Biases in Historical Data. Potential biases in the historical data include survivorship bias, transaction and tax costs, and the mixing of expected and unexpected components of past returns.

- *Survival bias.* Brown, Goetzmann, and Ross (1995) argued that the historical equity premium calculated using US data is likely to overstate the true (expected) premium because the US stock market turned out to be the most successful in world history. However, Dimson, Marsh, and Staunton (2008) examined stock and bond returns using data from 1900 to 2005 for 17 countries and concluded that the historical equity premium obtained for the United States is comparable to that of other countries.

- *Transaction costs, regulations, and taxes.* McGrattan and Prescott (2001) suggested that the high historical equity premium is mainly due to a large run-up in the equity price caused by the sharp decline in the tax rate on dividends. In their article, they claimed that the equity premium is less than 1% after accounting for taxes, regulations, and costs. To this result, I would add that index funds were not available to investors over the long periods studied by historical researchers; thus, equity investors earned returns lower than those of the index by the amount of (1) the explicit transaction and holding costs involved in forming portfolios and (2) the implicit cost of not being diversified.

- *Unanticipated repricing of equities.* Bernstein (1997) suggested that because equities started the sample period (which begins in 1926) at a price-to-earnings ratio of about 10 and ended the period at a P/E of about 20, the actual return on equities was higher than investors expected or required. Thus, the historical return overstates the future expected return. This finding was bolstered by Fama and French (2002), who used the DDM to show that investors expected an equity risk premium of about 3%, on average, from 1926 to the present.

Improvements in the Theoretical Model. The second broad category of research on the equity risk premium is a large body of literature exploring a variety of improvements in the original Mehra and Prescott (1985) model.

- *Rare events.* Rietz (1988) suggested that the ERP puzzle can be solved by incorporating a very small probability of a very large drop in consumption. If such a probability exists, the predicted equity premium would be large (to compensate investors for the small risk of a very bad outcome). Mehra and Prescott (1988) countered that, even if investors have a risk aversion parameter of 10, substantially larger than what they are generally believed to have, Rietz's model requires a 1 in 100 chance of a 25% decline in consumption, which they say has not happened in the United States. The largest aggregate consumption decline in the last 100 years, according to these authors, was only 8.8%.

I would remind these debaters that, according to Cooper and John, in the United States "from 1929 to 1933, real GDP decreased by 26.5 percent, while consumption decreased by 18.2 percent" (p. 1059).[9] Mehra and Prescott's (1988) 8.8% was the consumption decline in *just one year* of a multiyear decline.

Campbell, Lo, and MacKinlay pointed out in 1997 that "the difficulty with Rietz's argument is that it requires not only an economic catastrophe, but one which affects stock market investors more seriously than investors in short-term debt instruments" (p. 311).[10] Barro (2006) extended Rietz's model and argued that it does provide a plausible resolution of the equity premium puzzle.

- *Borrowing constraints and life-cycle issues.* Constantinides, Donaldson, and Mehra (2002) introduced life-cycle and borrowing constraints into the debate. They argued that as the correlation of equities with personal income changes over the life of an investor, so too does the attractiveness of equities to that investor. The young, who should borrow to smooth consumption and to invest in equities, cannot do so. Therefore, equities are priced almost exclusively by middle-aged investors, who find them—or at one time found them—to be unattractive. Thus, equities are underpriced and bonds are overpriced, producing a higher ERP than the puzzle literature predicts.

- *Behavioral concerns.* A large swath of behavioral finance literature argues that the combination of "myopic" loss aversion and narrow framing can help to resolve the equity premium puzzle. This category includes Benartzi

[9]Russell Cooper and Andrew John, *Theory and Applications of Economics* (v. 1.0): https://2012books.lardbucket.org/pdfs/theory-and-applications-of-economics.pdf.
[10]John Y. Campbell, Andrew W. Lo, and A. Craig MacKinlay, *The Econometrics of Financial Markets* (Princeton, NJ: Princeton University Press, 1997).

and Thaler (1995); Barberis, Huang, and Santos (2001); and Barberis and Huang (2007).

Time-Varying Premia and the DDM Counterrevolution

In one of the sharpest academic–practitioner divides in memory, some academics still consider the ERP puzzle literature relevant while almost no practitioners do. In addition, the future-equals-past method is rarely used by sophisticated practitioners and shows up mostly in the marketing literature of private wealth advisers who are trying to sell equities. So the DDM-based approach has been the only one with any real traction since the turn of the millennium.

While some practitioners had long used DDM-type estimates of the ERP, Campbell and Shiller, in the late 1980s, were really the first to reestablish the DDM as a respectable challenger to the then-dominant future-equals-past method. Their work spawned a vast literature that is exclusively forward looking; that is, it focuses on the expected rather than the realized ERP. This literature asserts that, like most DDM estimates, the ERP is time varying and countercyclical: The ERP is high when the market is low, and vice versa.

As noted earlier, the future-equals-past method, in contrast, is procyclical: It paradoxically gives higher forecasts after each market move upward and lower forecasts after each move downward. (An interesting contrast of investors' procyclical views with the DDM's countercyclical forecasts is presented in Greenwood and Shleifer [2014].)

This procyclicality proved to be the method's undoing. As of 1999, it was forecasting a greater than 12% annual return—an absurdity given the already bubble-like level of the market. So, around that time, the popularity of the future-equals-past method waned and acceptance of the DDM and allied approaches grew. Because the DDM had also been the preeminent method before Ibbotson and Sinquefield, I refer to this shift in thinking as the DDM counterrevolution.[11]

Valuation Levels and Subsequent Stock Returns. Campbell and Shiller (1988) "found that valuation ratios are positively correlated with subsequent returns and that the implied predictability of returns is substantial at longer horizons" (Campbell 2007, p. 1). So much for perfectly efficient

[11]To Ibbotson's credit, he has coauthored several papers that embrace—or, in the case of Diermeier, Ibbotson, and Siegel (1984), foreshadow—the DDM counterrevolution, in a sense overturning his own prior work with Sinquefield. See Roger G. Ibbotson and Peng Chen, "Long-Run Stock Returns: Participating in the Real Economy," *Financial Analysts Journal*, vol. 59, no. 1 (January/February 2003): 88–98; and Straehl and Ibbotson (2017).

markets! If returns can be predicted from valuation levels, then return expectations are not, or should not be, constant; thus (holding the riskless rate constant), the ERP is not constant either. There is information in valuation levels, then, that is potentially useful for timing the market and almost certainly useful for making periodic adjustments to the ERP assumption used in asset allocation and long-range planning.

Around that time, Fama and French (1988) came to a similar conclusion. They found that dividend yields were positively related to expected stock returns. This is the same as saying that high valuations (low dividend yields—that is, high price-to-dividend ratios) portend low stock returns and vice versa.

Once Jeremy Siegel (1994) and Peter Bernstein (1997), both best-selling authors with strong academic credentials, jumped decisively on the DDM bandwagon (see the discussion of Bernstein's work above), other works pursuing the same theme came in a flood. They include Campbell and Shiller (1998); Arnott and Bernstein (2002); Shiller (2000); Asness (2000, 2003); and Fama and French (2002; mentioned earlier in the puzzle discussion). As the field matured, other, more integrative works were produced, including Cochrane (2011) and Ilmanen (2011).

Two Influential Books. Among practitioners, the most influential of these works were Siegel's and Shiller's books, respectively titled *Stocks for the Long Run* (1994) and *Irrational Exuberance* (2000). Sometimes portrayed as rivals, the two authors are actually close personal friends who have vacationed together with their families and who enjoy debating the fine points of their views on markets.

- *CAPE method.* Shiller's book, in particular, has spawned a literature on the valuation method it espouses, called CAPE (cyclically adjusted price-to-earnings ratio). The CAPE literature is relevant to ERP estimation because CAPE is just an "improved" P/E—which, under carefully constrained conditions, is the inverse of the real expected return on a stock or stock portfolio.

Thus, if the CAPE or P/E of a portfolio (say, an index) is 25, the real expected return is 1/25 = 4%, and one can then subtract the real riskless rate (say, 1%, which is roughly the rate as of this writing) to arrive at the ERP (in this example, 3%). Jeremy Siegel (2016) set forth a constructive critique of the CAPE method, noting that researchers should emphasize more recent data, rather than the entire history, because accounting for the goodwill component of corporate earnings became more conservative around 1990. Adjusting for the accounting change raises the equity premium forecast.

- *Market timing.* As suggested above, if the ERP is time varying, then of course one could use that information to time the market. For obvious reasons, the literature on market timing intersects with the literature on estimating the value of the ERP at a given time. Ilmanen (2016) focused on the time-varying aspect of the ERP and other risk premia. While market timing per se is outside the scope of this review, his study also deals with long-term expectations, so it is included here.

Cash Flow to the Investor

The "payout" or "cash flow to the investor" literature relies on Miller and Modigliani,[12] whose work implies that, in the words of Straehl and Ibbotson (2017), "investors should be indifferent about whether they receive distributions via dividends or buybacks as well as how they participate in a buyback—that is, by receiving cash from tendering their shares or by receiving an increased proportion in the company" (p. 2). If this is the case, then explicit (cash) dividends are irrelevant and only total cash payout to the investor, including buybacks as well as dividends, is relevant for equity valuation. Diermeier, Ibbotson, and Siegel (1984) rely on this principle, as do Grinold and Kroner (2002) and Grinold, Kroner, and Siegel (2011).

Grinold's studies adjust dividends for "net new issues"—that is, the number of shares issued by companies in secondary public offerings *minus* the number of shares retired through buybacks and other corporate actions. This method brings together (1) the payout literature and (2) the dilution analysis performed by Bernstein and Arnott (2003), wherein the authors find that in order to achieve the earnings growth that has been observed, shareholders have had to suffer dilution amounting to a large 2% per year—with "dilution" referring to a decrease in the ownership percentage of a company represented by a given number of shares. This dilution, if continued in the future, will reduce the ERP.

But Straehl and Ibbotson (2017) were the first to really complete the payout analysis. They show that total payouts—in their formulation, dividends plus buybacks, not dividends alone—explain long-run stock market returns.[13] They proposed a new valuation measure, CATY (cyclically adjusted total yield), analogous to CAPE but constructed from "total yield" (payouts) rather than earnings, that "predicts changes in expected returns at least as well as the . . . CAPE" (p. 32). (The analysis is still not quite complete because total

[12]Merton H. Miller and Franco Modigliani, "Dividend Policy, Growth, and the Valuation of Shares," *Journal of Business*, vol. 34, no. 4 (October 1961): 411–433.

[13]In an article in progress, I argue that cash takeovers are a form of buyback and should be added to the total payout calculation.

yield should include cash takeovers as well as dividends and buybacks, but the authors did not have data for cash takeovers.)

As with the CAPE literature, the payout or CATY literature ties back to the ERP because the ERP can be calculated simply by subtracting the bond or bill yield from whatever expected total return on the stock market is implied by the CAPE or CATY analysis. Estimating the ERP and estimating the expected stock market return are essentially the same problem, because the two estimates differ by an observable constant (the riskless rate of return).

Yet the payout literature is contentious because that analysis relies on a satisfactory disentangling of earnings, earnings per share, number of shares, new issues, dilution, dividends, retained earnings, buybacks, and takeovers. These concepts, governed by accounting identities, seem easy until one tries to interpret them for the purpose of estimating expected returns and the ERP. Then they become difficult. While analysts perform this intricate analysis for individual companies with DCF models (by constructing measures such as EBITDA), such an approach may be daunting in the aggregate. In an inversion of the classic framework, where dividends are easy to forecast and capital gains hard, the payout literature shows that even the income part of the return, of which dividends are a key element, is subject to interpretation and controversy.

Why the increased interest in payout? Brav, Graham, Harvey, and Michaely (2005) reported that a 1982 change in SEC rules reduced the legal risk of repurchases. Since that time, dividend yields have fallen and buybacks have soared. In particular, "managers behave as if there is a significant capital market penalty associated with cutting dividends, but not with reducing repurchases. Accordingly, dividends are set conservatively and repurchases are used to absorb variation in total payout."[14] The resulting increase in buybacks makes it important to measure them as part of total payout rather than relying, as analysts in the last century generally did, on dividends.

Other Methods

This review of ERP estimation methods is not exhaustive. Duarte and Rosa (2015), making one-year rather than long-term forecasts, catalogued 20 models and found "that an optimal weighted average of all models places the one-year-ahead ERP in June 2012 at 12.2 percent, close to levels reached in the mid- and late 1970s, when the ERP was highest in the study sample."[15] This

[14]Bradford Cornell, Robert D. Arnott, and Max Moroz, "The Equity Premium Revisited" (1 February 2009): 4–5 (https://ssrn.com/abstract=1651196).
[15]From the authors' published abstract.

forecast was roughly correct over the subsequent five years, but it is way too high as a long-term expectation. This result suggests that Duarte and Rosa's method might be used for making the medium-term forecasts needed for dynamic or tactical asset allocation (timing) decisions.

An alternative approach to estimating the ERP is to look at credit markets. Equities per se don't have observable expected returns, but equity-like risky bonds do; the expected return is the yield minus an allowance for defaults. (The default allowance must necessarily be an estimate or forecast.) Extrapolating the risk–return relationship for credit bonds up to the risk or beta of equities can lead to a usable ERP number.

The literature on this question is well represented by Berg and Kaserer (2013), who used credit default swap (CDS) spreads instead of bond yields because of their greater accuracy. The authors' results for the US ERP range from 5.16% in 2004 to 7.18% in 2005; they note that, while the forecasts are high, these are upper limits, not midpoint estimates.

International Issues

The first efforts at measuring long-run equity returns in global markets were by Ibbotson, Siegel, and Love (1985) and Brinson, Diermeier, and Schlarbaum (1986). But neither of these studies explicitly estimated an ERP (although they made such estimation possible using a future-equals-past method). It took until the turn of the millennium for academics to focus their attention on the global equity market and its risk premium in a meaningful way.

Jorion and Goetzmann (1999) tested the concept of survival bias, which asserts that ERP estimates taken from successful countries, such as the United States and the United Kingdom, are upwardly biased because one could not know at the beginning of the period studied which countries' markets would survive and which would fail, or almost fail, due to war, nationalization, or other factors. This potential bias is a key issue in the estimation of any variable from observed historical data.

The authors

> collect a database of capital appreciation indexes for 39 markets going back into the 1920s. Over 1921 to 1996, the U.S. had the highest real return of all countries, at 4.3%, versus a median of 0.8% for other countries. The high equity premium obtained for the U.S. therefore seems to be the exception rather than the rule. (from the published abstract)

Dimson, Marsh, and Staunton (2002, 2017) have a slightly different take on survival bias. They documented, for a large assortment of countries, the annual returns on equities, bonds, and bills over a very long period: 1900 to the present. They also documented exchange rates and inflation rates so that real returns can be compared across countries. Like Jorion and Goetzmann (1999), they showed that survival bias is a significant factor in interpreting historical equity returns: An index composed of countries that survived the 20th century, with its wars and nationalizations, outperformed an unbiased index composed of countries that had markets in 1900.

However, the United States—one of the highest-returning markets—outperformed other surviving markets by only a modest margin. Equities, representing aggressive bets on the future, had the best returns in every country, representing the "triumph of the optimists" over pessimists who sought, through fixed-income investing, to defend their wealth positions against unforeseen disasters. Thus, survival bias is not as large a factor as one might naively guess.

Jeremy Siegel (1994) also weighed in on survival bias, noting that stocks beat bonds even in countries where markets were almost extinguished by war and inflation. In Germany and Japan, for example, stocks survived but bonds were ruined entirely.

Literature Reviews, Compilations, and Other Aggregative Works

CFA Institute Efforts. In 2002, the Association for Investment Management and Research (now CFA Institute) convened a group of academic and practitioner experts on the equity risk premium and published the ensuing discussion (AIMR 2002, online only). The discussion participants' estimates of the ERP ranged from 0.0% to 5.0%, excluding the results of a survey of finance professors who were asked what ERP estimate they used in their class materials; those estimates ranged as high as 7%. The average of the estimates made by the discussion participants was 3.7%.

Hammond, Leibowitz, and Siegel (2011) documented a reconvening of the AIMR (2002) group, this time by the CFA Institute Research Foundation, with some additions and deletions of participants. Several of the individual articles in the 2011 publication are referenced separately in this review. Remarkably, in the decade since the previous convocation, the experts' ERP estimates had converged tightly to 4%, plus or minus a small amount.

Additional Contributions. Additional elements of the ERP literature include Goetzmann and Ibbotson (2006); Campbell (2007); DeLong and Magin (2009); Cochrane (2011); Damodaran (2016); and Song (2007). Goetzmann and Ibbotson's book, *The Equity Risk Premium*, is an indispensable collection of the two Yale professors' works, with many coauthors, over more than 40 years. Several of the articles collected there are referenced separately in the bibliography below. Song (2007), the predecessor to this review, emphasizes the puzzle more than I have and is a valuable reference for readers interested in covering that literature in greater detail.

Conclusion

It is important to study and estimate the equity risk premium because it underpins some of the most significant financial and investment decisions a person or organization can make. Because the ERP cannot be observed directly, it must be estimated using one of a number of indirect approaches or models.

ERP models have gone through a number of fashions, sometimes called *regimes*, since the idea of estimating the ERP first came to prominence almost a half century ago. Initially, estimates of the equity risk premium, arrived at casually, tended to be low. Then, in the 1970s, Ibbotson and Sinquefield launched a period in which the ERP was expected to be high. This period lasted between a decade and a quarter century, depending on when one considers the DDM counterrevolution to have become fully established. Since the counterrevolution, the DDM approach seems to have prevailed and low to moderate estimates of the ERP have predominated.

What will happen in the future? While no one knows for certain, a low-return environment, sustained for a long enough time, creates the conditions for a high-return environment. But those conditions have not emerged yet. Market prices and valuation ratios suggest that low to moderate expected equity risk premia will prevail for some time.

I wish to thank P. Brett Hammond, research leader at Capital Group (Los Angeles), for his top-level editorial assistance and suggestions. Zhiyi Song, CFA, PhD, allowed me to recycle some of the ideas and language in The Equity Risk Premium: An Annotated Bibliography *(CFA Institute Research Foundation, 2007), which is the predecessor to this review; the section on the equity premium puzzle is mostly his (although I have shortened it), as are many of the annotations. I also thank various anonymous interviewees, including some whose work is cited herein.*

Bibliography

AIMR. 2002. *Equity Risk Premium Forum*. Charlottesville, VA: Association for Investment Management and Research.

This online resource consists of the proceedings of a high-level discussion group convened by AIMR (now CFA Institute) in 2001. Contributors include, in alphabetical order, Robert Arnott, Clifford Asness, Bradford Cornell, Campbell Harvey, Martin Leibowitz, Rajnish Mehra, Robert Shiller, Jeremy Siegel, and Richard Thaler.

Arnott, Robert D., and Peter L. Bernstein. 2002. "What Risk Premium Is 'Normal'?" *Financial Analysts Journal*, vol. 58, no. 2 (March/April): 64–85.

The expected equity return equals the dividend yield plus dividend growth plus the expected change in valuation, if any. As of year-end 1925, investors expected about 5.1% (about 1.4% more than the bond yield). The subsequent positive surprise was the result of four historical accidents: (1) Bonds had unanticipated losses; (2) valuations quadrupled, as measured by the price-to-dividend ratio (P/D); (3) the market survived; and (4) accelerated growth in real dividends and earnings occurred because of regulatory reform. These observations are used to construct a framework for estimating the equity risk premium at each point in time, including the present. The "normal" equity risk premium, or historical average of what investors were actually expecting, is 2.4%, and the current (2002) equity risk premium is around zero.

Asness, Clifford S. 2000. "Stocks versus Bonds: Explaining the Equity Risk Premium." *Financial Analysts Journal*, vol. 56, no. 2 (March/April): 96–113.

Changes in the expected equity risk premium are explained by changes in the relative volatilities of the two assets (stocks and bonds). The low ERP at the time of this study is consistent with low volatility in the stock market and high volatility in the bond market. The author writes, "This model fits 1871–1998 data extremely well" (p. 96). Interestingly, this finding holds over periods (before modern times) when volatility was not widely measured or understood to be a factor in asset returns.

Asness, Clifford S. 2003. "Fight the Fed Model." *Journal of Portfolio Management*, vol. 30, no. 1 (Fall): 11–24.

The "Fed model," so called because the US Federal Reserve has sometimes used it to assess market valuation levels, compares the earnings yield (E/P, the reciprocal of P/E) on a stock market index to the yield on Treasury bonds. Asness argues that the model is incorrect because it mixes real and nominal quantities. Corporate earnings are "real," varying with inflation, and bonds are nominal. Thus, the proper comparison is between earnings yields and *real* interest rates.

Barberis, Nicholas, and Ming Huang. 2007. "The Loss Aversion/Narrow Framing Approach to the Equity Premium Puzzle." In *Handbook of the Equity Risk Premium*. Edited by Rajnish Mehra. Amsterdam: Elsevier.

The authors review the behavioral approach to understanding the ERP puzzle. The key elements of this approach are loss aversion and narrow framing, two well-known features of decision making under risk in experimental settings. By incorporating these features into traditional utility functions, Barberis and Huang show that a large equity premium and a low and stable risk-free rate can be generated simultaneously, even when consumption growth is smooth and only weakly correlated with the stock market.

Barberis, Nicholas, Ming Huang, and Tano Santos. 2001. "Prospect Theory and Asset Prices." *Quarterly Journal of Economics*, vol. 116, no. 1 (February): 1–53.

This article proposes a new approach for pricing assets by incorporating two psychological ideas into the traditional consumption-based model. Investors are assumed to be more sensitive to losses than to gains, and their risk aversion changes over time depending on their prior investment outcomes. The authors show that this framework can help explain the high historical equity risk premium.

Barro, Robert. 2006. "Rare Disasters and Asset Markets in the Twentieth Century." *Quarterly Journal of Economics*, vol. 121, no. 3 (August): 823–866.

This article extends the analysis of Rietz (1988) and argues that it does provide a plausible resolution of the ERP puzzle. Barro suggests that the rare-disasters framework (i.e., the allowance for low-probability disasters proposed by Rietz) can explain the ERP puzzle while "maintaining the tractable framework of a representative agent, time-additive and iso-elastic preferences, and complete markets" (p. 823). These technical terms refer to assumptions that are embedded in Mehra and Prescott (1985) and that are considered standard in general equilibrium or macroeconomic models.

Benartzi, Shlomo, and Richard H. Thaler. 1995. "Myopic Loss Aversion and the Equity Premium Puzzle." *Quarterly Journal of Economics*, vol. 110, no. 1 (February): 73–92.

This article proposes an explanation for the equity premium based on two concepts from the psychology of decision making. The first concept is "loss aversion," the tendency for investors to be more sensitive to losses than to gains. The second concept is "mental accounting," whereby investors mentally separate their portfolios into subportfolios for which they may have quite different utility functions or risk aversion parameters. For example, investors may have one set of portfolios that they never evaluate and another set that they evaluate every day. Benartzi and Thaler show that the size of the historical equity premium can be explained if investors evaluate their portfolios at least annually.

Berg, Tobias, and Christoph Kaserer. 2013. "Extracting the Equity Premium from CDS Spreads." *Journal of Derivatives*, vol. 21, no. 1 (Fall): 8–26.

Credit default swap spreads can be used to estimate the ERP because they are the directly observable market price of corporate performance risk, while equity expected returns are not directly observable and must be inferred. The authors' estimates of the ERP are high, ranging from 5% to over 7%, but they caution that because of their assumptions, these should be regarded as upper limits, not best estimates.

Bernstein, Peter L. 1997. "What Rate of Return Can You Reasonably Expect . . . or What Can the Long Run Tell Us about the Short Run?" *Financial Analysts Journal*, vol. 53, no. 2 (March/April): 20–28.

By studying historical intervals when stock valuation (price/dividends or price/earnings) was the same at the end of the interval as at the beginning, one can avoid incorporating unexpected valuation changes into long-term rate of return studies. The analysis gives an equity risk premium of 3%, although the more interesting finding is that equity returns are mean reverting whereas bond returns have no mean to which to revert. Thus, in the very long run and in real terms, stocks are safer than bonds.

Bernstein, William J., and Robert D. Arnott. 2003. "Earnings Growth: The Two Percent Dilution." *Financial Analysts Journal*, vol. 59, no. 5 (September/October): 47–55.

This essential paper is best described in the authors' abstract: "Two important concepts played a key role in the bull market of the 1990s. . . . First, many investors believed that earnings could grow faster than the macroeconomy.

In fact, earnings must grow slower than GDP because the growth of existing enterprises contributes only part of GDP growth; the role of entrepreneurial capitalism, the creation of new enterprises, is a key driver of GDP growth, and it does not contribute to the growth in earnings and dividends of existing enterprises. During the 20th century, growth in stock prices and dividends [not per share but in absolute magnitude] was 2 percent [per year] less than underlying macroeconomic growth. Second, many investors believed that stock buybacks would permit earnings to grow faster than GDP. The important metric [for evaluating the impact of share buybacks on earnings per share] is not the volume of buybacks, however, but net buybacks—stock buybacks less new share issuance. . . . We demonstrate . . . that during the 20th century, new share issuance in many nations almost always exceeded stock buybacks by an average of 2 percent or more a year" (p. 47).

Brav, Alon, John R. Graham, Campbell R. Harvey, and Roni Michaely. 2005. "Payout Policy in the 21st Century." *Journal of Financial Economics*, vol. 77, no. 3 (September): 483–527.

The authors trace the recent boom in share buybacks, as opposed to cash dividends, to a change in SEC rules in 1982 and find that dividends are managed conservatively (because there is a financial market penalty for cutting them) while buybacks are managed discretionarily (because there does not seem to be any such penalty for reducing buybacks).

Brinson, Gary P., Jeffrey J. Diermeier, and Gary G. Schlarbaum. 1986. "A Composite Portfolio Benchmark for Pension Plans." *Financial Analysts Journal*, vol. 42, no. 2 (March/April): 15–24.

The authors calculate returns on a global multi-asset portfolio, using fixed weights, and recommend it as a benchmark for pension plans. This study is one of the first attempts to measure the return on world wealth, although the use of fixed weights means that the portfolio manager would have to transact in order to rebalance to these weights, instead of pursuing a buy-and-hold strategy. The use of fixed weights avoids the need to monitor the portfolio for excessive risk caused by one asset class becoming dominant over time.

Brown, Stephen J., William N. Goetzmann, and Stephen A. Ross. 1995. "Survival." *Journal of Finance*, vol. 50, no. 3 (July): 853–873.

This article suggests that survival bias could induce a substantial spurious equity premium and at least partially explain the equity premium puzzle documented by Mehra and Prescott (1985)—that is, explain it away, because the returns used to frame the puzzle were neither expected nor achieved by many investors.

Campbell, John Y. 2007. "Estimating the Equity Premium." NBER Working Paper 13423 (http://www.nber.org/papers/w13423.pdf).

In this extended literature review and personal essay, Campbell finds that "the world geometric average equity premium was almost 4% at the end of March 2007, implying a world arithmetic average equity premium somewhat above 5%. Both valuation ratios and the cross-section of stock prices imply that the equity premium fell considerably in the late 20th Century, but has risen modestly in the early years of the 21st Century" (published abstract).

Campbell, John H., and Robert J. Shiller. 1988. "Stock Prices, Earnings, and Expected Dividends." *Journal of Finance*, vol. 43, no. 3 (July): 661–676.

In what is almost certainly the first "CAPE" paper, the authors write that "a long moving average of real earnings helps to forecast future real dividends. The ratio of this earnings variable to the current stock price is a powerful predictor of the return on stock, particularly . . . over several years" (p. 675). Thus, contrary to the efficient market hypothesis, which prevailed in academia at the time this paper was written, stock prices are at least somewhat predictable and countercyclical; that is, expected returns are high when prices (relative to earnings and dividends) are low and low when prices are high.

Campbell, John Y., and Robert J. Shiller. 1998. "Valuation Ratios and the Long-Run Stock Market Outlook." *Journal of Portfolio Management*, vol. 24, no. 2 (Winter): 11–26.

According to the efficient market hypothesis, the dividend-to-price ratio (D/P) can forecast changes in dividends or changes in price or both. Empirically, it forecasts only changes in price. At the then-current (1998) D/P, the forecast was extraordinarily bearish: The stock market was expected to lose about two-thirds of its real value. The forecast becomes less drastically bearish (although still quite bearish) when one uses total cash payout (i.e., dividends plus share buybacks), earnings, the 10-year moving average of earnings in constant dollars, or other variables instead of dividends in the denominator. Real stock returns close to zero over the next 10 years were forecast. A number of statistical weaknesses in the analysis are acknowledged: The historical observations are not independent, and the analysis depends on valuation ratios regressing to their historical means, whereas the actual means are not known and could conceivably lie outside the historical range.

Cochrane, John H. 2011. "Presidential Address: Discount Rates." *Journal of Finance*, vol. 66, no. 4 (August): 1047–1108.

This presidential address to the American Finance Association focuses on changing beliefs in the field of finance. Cochrane indicates that discount-rate variation, including variation in the ERP, "is the central organizing question of current asset-pricing research." He describes the impact of incorporating discount-rate variation on "portfolio theory, accounting, cost of capital, capital structure, compensation, and macroeconomics" (p. 1047).

Constantinides, George M., John B. Donaldson, and Rajnish Mehra. 2002. "Junior Can't Borrow: A New Perspective on the Equity Premium Puzzle." *Quarterly Journal of Economics*, vol. 117, no. 1 (February): 269–296.

As the correlation of equities with personal income changes over the life of an investor, so does the attractiveness of equities to that investor. The young, who should borrow to smooth consumption and to invest in equities, cannot do so. Therefore, equities are priced almost exclusively by middle-aged investors, who find equities to be unattractive. The result is a decreased demand for equities and an increased demand for bonds relative to what would be the case in a perfectly competitive market.

Damodaran, Aswath. 2016. "Equity Risk Premiums (ERP): Determinants, Estimation and Implications—The 2016 Edition" (5 March): https://ssrn.com/abstract=2742186.

In an annually updated comprehensive review, Damodaran catalogues the various methods available for estimating the ERP, including "economic determinants of equity risk premiums," the standard historical approach, the survey approach, and "the implied approach, where a forward-looking estimate of the premium is estimated using either current equity prices or risk premiums in non-equity markets." Damodaran also looks at "the relationship between the equity risk premium and risk premiums in the bond market . . . and in real estate . . . and how that relationship can be mined to [generate] expected equity risk premiums" (p. 2).

DeLong, J. Bradford, and Konstantin Magin. 2009. "The U.S. Equity Return Premium: Past, Present, and Future." *Journal of Economic Perspectives*, vol. 23, no. 1 (Winter): 193–208.

In this sophisticated literature review and general discussion, the authors state reasons why others have found a puzzle or macroeconomic paradox in the high expected returns of equity markets and present accumulated evidence that equity returns have been and will continue to be high relative to riskless assets such as Treasury bills.

Diermeier, Jeffrey J., Roger G. Ibbotson, and Laurence B. Siegel. 1984. "The Supply of Capital Market Returns." *Financial Analysts Journal*, vol. 40, no. 2 (March/April): 74–80.

Stock total returns must equal dividend yields plus the growth rate of dividends, which cannot, in the long run, exceed the growth rate of the economy. If infinite-run expected dividend growth exceeded infinite-run expected economic growth, then dividends would crowd out all other economic claims. Net new issues, representing new capital (transferred from the labor market) that is needed so the corporate sector can grow, may cause the dividend growth rate to be lower than the GDP growth rate. Thus, the equity risk premium equals the dividend yield (minus new issues net of share buybacks) plus the GDP growth rate minus the riskless rate.

The "supply side" or "supply model" thread begins with this work, which was written when so-called supply-side economics was popular; the authors strove to apply supply-oriented thinking to investment questions.

Dimson, Elroy, Paul Marsh, and Mike Staunton. 2002. *Triumph of the Optimists: 101 Years of Global Investment Returns*. Princeton, NJ: Princeton University Press.

The authors document the annual returns on equities, bonds, bills, currencies, and inflation over the 20th century for all major markets (the United States, the United Kingdom, Japan, France, Germany, Canada, Italy, Spain, Switzerland, Australia, the Netherlands, Sweden, Belgium, Ireland, Denmark, and South Africa). Later editions include more countries. The authors show that survival bias is a significant factor in estimating future returns because past returns reflect only those countries that have been successful. In a speech, Dimson summarized his and his coauthors' work as follows: "Although equities gave the highest return in every country, they were also risky, and we demonstrate the importance of diversifying globally as well as across asset classes" (p. 1).[16]

[16]Elroy Dimson, "Triumph of the Optimists," Arrowstreet Capital (October 2003): http://csinvesting.org/wp-content/uploads/2015/03/2781_triumph_of_the_optimists.pdf.

Dimson, Elroy, Paul Marsh, and Mike Staunton. 2008. "The Worldwide Equity Premium: A Smaller Puzzle." In *Handbook of the Equity Risk Premium*. Edited by Rajnish Mehra. Amsterdam: Elsevier.

Using 1900–2005 data for 17 countries, the authors show that the annualized equity premium for the rest of the world was 4.2%, not too much below the US equity premium of 5.5% over the same period.

The historical equity premium is decomposed into dividend growth, multiple expansion, the dividend yield, and changes in the real exchange rate. Assuming zero change in the real exchange rate, no multiple expansion, and a dividend yield 0.5%–1% lower than the historical mean of 4.49%, the authors forecast an equity premium on the world index of about 3%–3.5% on a geometric mean basis and 4.5%–5% on an arithmetic mean basis.

Dimson, Elroy, Paul Marsh, and Mike Staunton. 2011. "Equity Premiums around the World." In *Rethinking the Equity Risk Premium*. Edited by P. Brett Hammond, Jr., Martin L. Leibowitz, and Laurence B. Siegel. Charlottesville, VA: CFA Institute Research Foundation.

While the authors document geometric mean realized equity risk premia ranging from 2.7% in Denmark to 6.7% in Australia over 1900–2009, they project lower returns going forward. Their estimate of the global ERP at the time of their writing was "3.4 percent for the average country and . . . 4.0 percent for the World index" (p. 47).

Dimson, Elroy, Paul Marsh, and Mike Staunton. 2017. *Credit Suisse Global Investment Returns Yearbook 2017: Summary Edition*. Zurich: Credit Suisse (https://publications.credit-suisse.com/tasks/render/file/?fileID=B8FDD84D-A4CD-D983-12840F52F61BA0B4).

This yearbook annually updates the data and analysis presented in Dimson, Marsh, and Staunton (2002).

Duarte, Fernando, and Carlo Rosa. 2015. "The Equity Risk Premium: A Review of Models." *Economic Policy Review*, vol. 21, no. 2 (December): 39–57 (https://ssrn.com/abstract=2886334).

These two Federal Reserve economists "categoriz[e] the [available] models into five classes: trailing historical mean, dividend discount, cross-sectional estimation, regression analysis using valuation ratios or macroeconomic variables, and surveys" (published abstract). They make a one-year-ahead ERP forecast (as of June 2012) of 12.2%.

Fama, Eugene F., and Kenneth R. French. 1988. "Dividend Yields and Expected Stock Returns." *Journal of Financial Economics*, vol. 22, no. 1 (October): 3–25.

Dividend yields predict intermediate- and long-horizon equity market returns much better than they do short-horizon returns. While regressions of returns on dividend yields typically explain less than 5% of monthly or quarterly return variances, the percentage explained rises to 25%–40% for a three- to five-year horizon. This result sharply contradicts the theory of efficient markets and suggests that investors should buy when dividend yields are high and sell when they are low.

Fama, Eugene F., and Kenneth R. French. 2002. "The Equity Premium." *Journal of Finance*, vol. 57, no. 2 (April): 637–659.

This article compares alternative estimates of the unconditional expected stock return between 1872 and 2000 and explains the low expected return estimates derived from fundamentals, such as dividends and earnings, for the 1951–2000 period. The authors conclude that the decline in discount rates largely caused the unexplained capital gain of the last half century.

Goetzmann, William N., and Roger G. Ibbotson. 2006. *The Equity Risk Premium: Essays and Explorations*. Oxford, UK: Oxford University Press.

This comprehensive volume includes the authors' works, with many coauthors, from the 1970s to the early 2000s. Because the authors produced much of the literature discussed in this review, this collection of Goetzmann and Ibbotson's works is indispensable for serious scholars of the equity risk premium and related issues.

Greenwood, Robin, and Andrei Shleifer. 2014. "Expectations of Returns and Expected Returns." *Review of Financial Studies*, vol. 27, no. 3 (March): 714–746 (https://scholar.harvard.edu/files/shleifer/files/expectations_of_returns_public._feb_2014_print.pdf).

Survey-based measures of the returns that investors expect are procyclical (they rise after markets have risen), while model-based estimates of expected returns are countercyclical (they fall after markets have risen). Thus, the returns that investors say they expect are negatively correlated with the returns they would expect if they followed the (mostly DDM-based) models.

Grinold, Richard C., and Kenneth F. Kroner. 2002. "The Equity Risk Premium: Analyzing the Long-Run Prospects for the Stock Market." *Investment Insights*, vol. 5, no. 3 (July).

This is the predecessor article to Grinold, Kroner, and Siegel (2011) and provides some detail on the input estimation methods not included in the later article.

Grinold, Richard C., Kenneth F. Kroner, and Laurence B. Siegel. 2011. "A Supply Model of the Equity Premium." In *Rethinking the Equity Risk Premium*. Edited by P. Brett Hammond, Jr., Martin L. Leibowitz, and Laurence B. Siegel. Charlottesville, VA: CFA Institute Research Foundation.

The authors examine separately the four components of the expected equity risk premium (income return, expected real earnings growth, expected inflation, and expected repricing) and suggest a then-current risk premium of about 3.6% over 10-year Treasury bonds. The authors also forcefully attack the "puzzle" literature, saying that they have never understood how one can seriously assert that the theory is right and the data are wrong.

Hammond, P. Brett, Jr., Martin L. Leibowitz, and Laurence B. Siegel, eds. 2011. *Rethinking the Equity Risk Premium*. Charlottesville, VA: CFA Institute Research Foundation.

In 2011, the CFA Institute Research Foundation reconvened the equity risk premium discussion group in AIMR (2002), with some changes to the participant list. Rather than a transcript of proceedings, this volume is a collection of articles submitted by the presenters after the meeting. The included contributors, in alphabetical order by lead author, are Andrew Ang and Xiaoyan Zhang; Robert D. Arnott; Clifford Asness; Peng Chen; Elroy Dimson, Paul Marsh, and Mike Staunton; Richard C. Grinold, Kenneth F. Kroner, and Laurence B. Siegel; P. Brett Hammond, Jr., and Martin L. Leibowitz; Roger G. Ibbotson; Antti Ilmanen; Rajnish Mehra; and Jeremy J. Siegel. Some of the individual articles are referenced separately in this review.

Ibbotson, Roger G., Roger J. Grabowski, James P. Harrington, and Carla Nunes. 2017. *2017 Stocks, Bonds, Bills, and Inflation (SBBI) Yearbook*. Hoboken, NJ: John Wiley & Sons.

This yearbook annually updates the data and analysis presented in Ibbotson and Sinquefield (1976).

Ibbotson, Roger G., Laurence B. Siegel, and Kathryn S. Love. 1985. "World Wealth: Market Values and Returns." *Journal of Portfolio Management*, vol. 12, no. 1 (Fall): 4–23.

The authors present annual return and market-capitalization data on global equities, global fixed income, commodity metals, and US real estate over 1960–1984. Cap-weighting the individual asset-class returns, they present a composite return series for the world market wealth portfolio. They note that what is omitted (human capital, non-US real estate, private businesses) is probably larger than what is included.

Ibbotson, Roger G., and Rex A. Sinquefield. 1976. "Stocks, Bonds, Bills, and Inflation: Year-by-Year Historical Returns (1926–1974)." *Journal of Business*, vol. 49, no. 1 (January): 11–47 (http://epge.fgv.br/we/MFEE/FinancasCorporativas/2011?action=AttachFile&do=get&target=Ibbotson.pdf).

Total equity returns consist of a stationary part (the equity risk premium) and a nonstationary part (the interest rate component, which consists of a real interest rate plus compensation for expected inflation). The estimator of the future arithmetic mean equity risk premium is the past arithmetic mean premium, which was about 7% when the authors wrote the article. To this is added the then-current interest rate, 4.8% (on 20-year Treasury bonds). The sum of these, about 12%, was the arithmetic mean expected total return on equities. The historical equity risk premium reflects equilibrium at all times and forms the proper estimator of the future equity risk premium. (Later updates discuss other methods rather than supporting a doctrinaire "future-equals-past" interpretation of historical data.)

Ilmanen, Antti. 2011. *Expected Returns: An Investor's Guide to Harvesting Market Rewards*. Hoboken, NJ: John Wiley & Sons.

The author takes a "cubic" approach to understanding expected returns. On one face of the cube are conventional asset classes: stocks, government bonds, credits, and alternatives. A second face represents trading strategies: value, "carry" (roughly speaking, yield), trend, and volatility. The third face is for underlying macroeconomic factors: growth, inflation, illiquidity, and tail risks. The treatment is encyclopedic and covers many aspects of return estimation, alpha generation, and beta-focused investing.

Ilmanen, Antti. 2016. "A Historical Perspective on Time-Varying Expected Returns." In *Financial Market History: Reflections on the Past for Investors*

Today. Edited by David Chambers and Elroy Dimson. Charlottesville, VA: CFA Institute Research Foundation.

The author focuses on the difficulty of timing the market using time-varying valuation or risk premium approaches but also engages in a very high-quality discussion of ERP issues in general.

Jorion, Philippe, and William N. Goetzmann. 1999. "Global Stock Markets in the Twentieth Century." *Journal of Finance*, vol. 54, no. 3: 953–980.

The authors compare real stock returns over 1921–1996 in the United States with real stock returns in 38 other countries over the same period and find that the US returns were much higher. Thus, survival bias is a significant factor in evaluating historical returns and the historical ERP. Simply projecting past returns forward into the future results in forecasts that are much too high.

McGrattan, Ellen R., and Edward C. Prescott. 2001. "Taxes, Regulations, and Asset Prices." NBER Working Paper 8623 (December): http://www.nber.org/papers/w8623.pdf.

The large run-up in equity value relative to GDP between 1962 and 2000 was mainly caused by (1) large reductions in individual tax rates, (2) increased opportunities to hold equity in nontaxed pension plans, and (3) increases in intangible and foreign capital. The authors argue that the high equity risk premium documented by Mehra and Prescott (1985) is not puzzling after these three factors are accounted for. However, in the future, one should expect no further gains from tax policy; the currently expected real return on equities is about 4%, down from 8% in the early postwar period.

Mehra, Rajnish. 2003. "The Equity Premium: Why Is It a Puzzle?" *Financial Analysts Journal*, vol. 59, no. 1 (January/February): 54–69.

The ERP puzzle literature is easily misunderstood because of its difficulty. Here, the puzzle is stated in language that is accessible to most finance practitioners. First, empirical facts regarding the returns and risks of major asset classes are presented. Then, the theory responsible for the puzzle is summarized. Modern asset-pricing theory assumes that economic agents pursue and, on average, get fair deals. When one follows this line of reasoning to its conclusion, using the tools of classic growth and real business cycle theory, an equity risk premium of at most 1% emerges. An extensive discussion reveals why this is the case and addresses various attempts made by other authors to resolve the puzzle.

Mehra, Rajnish, and Edward C. Prescott. 1985. "The Equity Premium: A Puzzle." *Journal of Monetary Economics*, vol. 15, no. 2 (March): 145–161.

In this respected work, Mehra and Prescott first document the "equity premium puzzle" using a consumption-based asset-pricing model in which the quantity of risk is defined as the covariance of excess stock return with consumption growth and the price of risk is the coefficient of relative risk aversion. Because of the low risk resulting from the smooth historical growth of consumption, the 6% ERP in the 1889–1978 period can be explained only by a very high coefficient of risk aversion in the magnitude of 30 to 40. Risk aversion parameters observed in other aspects of financial behavior are around 1. Such a risk aversion parameter is consistent with at most a 1% equity risk premium and possibly one as small as 0.25%.

Note that Mehra and Prescott assumed that consumption was equal to aggregate dividends. Because consumption is very smooth and dividends are not as smooth, this comparison may be troublesome.

Mehra, Rajnish, and Edward C. Prescott. 1988. "The Equity Premium: A Solution?" *Journal of Monetary Economics*, vol. 22, no. 1 (July): 133–136.

This article is a response to Rietz (1988).

Rietz, Thomas A. 1988. "The Equity Risk Premium: A Solution." *Journal of Monetary Economics*, vol. 22, no. 1 (July): 117–131.

Rietz suggests that the ERP puzzle can be solved by incorporating a very small probability of a very large drop in consumption. In such a scenario, the risk-free rate is much lower than the equity return. In an article published in the same issue of the *Journal of Monetary Economics*, Mehra and Prescott (1988) argue that, in Rietz's model, "with a 1-in-100 chance of a 25 percent decline in consumption, the required risk aversion parameter is 10" (p. 135). However, these authors say, the largest consumption decline in the last 100 years was only 8.8%.

But during the Great Depression, the stock market fell by 86% from peak to trough and dividends fell by about half; aggregate consumption in the economy, not just by stockholders, fell by about 18%. Mehra and Prescott's 8.8% is the largest one-year decline in a multiyear consumption decline.

Shiller, Robert J. 2000. *Irrational Exuberance*. Princeton, NJ: Princeton University Press.

Irrational Exuberance, the title taken from an Alan Greenspan speech, presents basic concepts of behavioral finance and argues that markets become overextended, so that returns can be above normal and then below normal for extended periods.

Shiller introduces (to a mass audience) the concept of the cyclically adjusted price-to-earnings ratio, or CAPE, which modifies the traditional P/E by using the average of 10 years' trailing real earnings in place of (trailing or forecast) current-year earnings. This method achieves a compromise, using a period longer than one year (to stabilize the earnings measure) but not too long (to exclude old, irrelevant data). The ability of the CAPE to make market return forecasts is documented.

Siegel, Jeremy J. 1994. *Stocks for the Long Run*. New York: McGraw-Hill.

This immensely influential book documents "Siegel's constant": The author argues that real (inflation-adjusted) returns on stocks have been close to a constant over very long time periods. "Note the extraordinary stability of the real return on stocks," the author writes, "over all major subperiods: 7.0 percent per year from 1802 through 1870, 6.6 percent from 1871 through 1925, and 7.2 percent per year since 1926" (p. 11). Even in countries where stock markets were almost destroyed by war, such as Germany and Japan, stocks beat bonds, which were entirely ruined in those countries.

Siegel, Jeremy J. 2016. "The Shiller CAPE Ratio: A New Look." *Financial Analysts Journal*, vol. 72, no. 3 (May/June): 41–50.

While generally supportive of Shiller's (2000) CAPE approach to market valuation, Siegel notes that accounting standards have become more conservative, especially with respect to depreciation requirements for goodwill. Thus, CAPE ratios from before these changes are not necessarily relevant for assessing the current valuation of the market. When more contemporary data are used, the market appears less overvalued.

The author also recommends using national income and product accounts (NIPA) profits as a check on S&P 500 or other corporate earnings series, because the earnings series reported by Standard & Poor's do not "observe consistent and uniform conventions across time" (p. 49).

Song, Zhiyi. 2007. *The Equity Risk Premium: An Annotated Bibliography*. Charlottesville, VA: CFA Institute Research Foundation.

This is the predecessor to the current review. Song covers most of the same issues I do, but from the vantage point of a decade earlier and with greater emphasis on the "puzzle" literature associated with Mehra and Prescott (1985).

Straehl, Philip U., and Roger G. Ibbotson. 2017. "The Long-Run Drivers of Stock Returns: Total Payouts and the Real Economy." *Financial Analysts Journal*, vol. 73, no. 3 (Third Quarter): 32–52.

The authors present evidence, over a 143-year period in the United States, that total payouts (dividends plus buybacks), not dividends alone or earnings, are "the key drivers of long-run stock market returns" (p. 32). They show that aggregate (not per share) total payouts have grown at the same rate as GDP on average over time. The authors also introduce the cyclically adjusted total yield—that is, yield based on 10 years' average real total payout—and show its ability to predict returns.

This article resolves a number of issues raised by Diermeier, Ibbotson, and Siegel (1984) and reconciles the DDM/DCF literature with the work of Miller and Modigliani,[17] who showed that investors should be indifferent between cash dividends and other forms of cash payout.

[17]See Note 12.

Named Endowments

The CFA Institute Research Foundation acknowledges with sincere gratitude the generous contributions of the Named Endowment participants listed below.

Gifts of at least US$100,000 qualify donors for membership in the Named Endowment category, which recognizes in perpetuity the commitment toward unbiased, practitioner-oriented, relevant research that these firms and individuals have expressed through their generous support of the CFA Institute Research Foundation.

Ameritech
Anonymous
Robert D. Arnott
Theodore R. Aronson, CFA
Asahi Mutual Life Insurance Company
Batterymarch Financial Management
Boston Company
Boston Partners Asset Management, L.P.
Gary P. Brinson, CFA
Brinson Partners, Inc.
Capital Group International, Inc.
Concord Capital Management
Dai-Ichi Life Company
Daiwa Securities
Mr. and Mrs. Jeffrey Diermeier
Gifford Fong Associates
Investment Counsel Association of America, Inc.
Jacobs Levy Equity Management
John A. Gunn, CFA
Jon L. Hagler Foundation
Long-Term Credit Bank of Japan, Ltd.
Lynch, Jones & Ryan, LLC
Meiji Mutual Life Insurance Company
Miller Anderson & Sherrerd, LLP
John B. Neff
Nikko Securities Co., Ltd.
Nippon Life Insurance Company of Japan
Nomura Securities Co., Ltd.
Payden & Rygel
Provident National Bank
Frank K. Reilly, CFA
Salomon Brothers
Sassoon Holdings Pte. Ltd.
Scudder Stevens & Clark
Security Analysts Association of Japan
Shaw Data Securities, Inc.
Sit Investment Associates, Inc.
Standish, Ayer & Wood, Inc.
State Farm Insurance Company
Sumitomo Life America, Inc.
T. Rowe Price Associates, Inc.
Templeton Investment Counsel Inc.
Frank Trainer, CFA
Travelers Insurance Co.
USF&G Companies
Yamaichi Securities Co., Ltd.

Senior Research Fellows

Financial Services Analyst Association

For more on upcoming Research Foundation publications and webcasts, please visit www.cfainstitute.org/learning/foundation.

Research Foundation monographs are online at www.cfapubs.org.

Encyclopedia of
COUNSELING

Who Else Wants To Say, "I Passed"?

With more questions and answers than any other edition, the *Encyclopedia of Counseling,* Fourth Edition, is still the only book you need to pass the NCE, CPCE, and other counseling exams. Every chapter has new and updated material and is still written in Dr. Rosenthal's lively, user-friendly style counselors know and love. The book's new and improved coverage incorporates a range of vital topics, including social media, group work in career counseling, private practice and nonprofit work, addictions, neurocounseling, research trends, the *DSM-5*, the new ACA and NBCC codes of ethics, and much, much more.

Howard Rosenthal, EdD, CCMHC, HS-BCP, LPC, MAC, NCC, is professor and coordinator of the human services program at St. Louis Community College at Florissant Valley and is the author of numerous successful publications on counseling, counselor training, test anxiety, and test preparation.

RESEARCH FOUNDATION CONTRIBUTION FORM

☑ **Yes**, I want the Research Foundation to continue to fund innovative research that advances the investment management profession. Please accept my tax-deductible contribution at the following level:

Thought Leadership Circle.................... US$1,000,000 or more
Named Endowment...................... US$100,000 to US$999,999
Research Fellow .... US$10,000 to US$99,999
Contributing Donor............................ US$1,000 to US$9,999
Friend .... Up to US$999

I would like to donate US$ ___________________.

☐ My check is enclosed (payable to the CFA Institute Research Foundation).
☐ I would like to donate appreciated securities (send me information).
☐ Please charge my donation to my credit card.
☐ VISA ☐ MC ☐ Amex ☐ Diners

Card Number

___/___ Expiration Date

______________________ Name on card PLEASE PRINT

☐ Corporate Card
☐ Personal Card

______________________ Signature

☐ This is a pledge. Please bill me for my donation of US$_____________
☐ I would like recognition of my donation to be:
☐ Individual donation ☐ Corporate donation ☐ Different individual

____
PLEASE PRINT NAME OR COMPANY NAME AS YOU WOULD LIKE IT TO APPEAR

PLEASE PRINT ☐ Mr. ☐ Mrs. ☐ Ms. MEMBER NUMBER ______________

Last Name (Family Name) First (Given Name) Middle Initial

Title

Address

City State/Province Country ZIP/Postal Code

Please mail this completed form with your contribution to:
The CFA Institute Research Foundation • P.O. Box 2082
Charlottesville, VA 22902-2082 USA

For more on the CFA Institute Research Foundation, please visit www.cfainstitute.org/learning/foundation/Pages/index.aspx.

Made in the USA
Monee, IL
04 November 2026

67382725R00022